THE MOSER GANG

BOB MOSER

Copyrighted Material

The Moser Gang © 2025 by Robert Moser.

All Rights Reserved.

No part of this publication may be reproduced, stored in a retrieval system or transmitted, in any form or by any means—electronic, mechanical, photocopying, recording or otherwise—without prior written permission from the publisher, except for the inclusion of brief quotations in a review.

ISBNs
Print: 979-8-218-62820-8

Published in the United States of America by
Good Seed Publishing Co.

Good Seed Ranch drawing by Sheila Hitchcock.

This book is dedicated to:
My fellow-members of the Moser Gang:
Craig Moser (Captain)
John Moser (Red Boots)
My cousins, Gary and Reid Moser

My children:
Hannah, Sayde, Andrew, and Rebekah
They heard these stories so many times over the years they could probably recite them in their sleep.

My first wife, Cindee,
who passed away in July of 2021.
She was married for 43 years to a man who never really outgrew his Moser Gang persona. She lovingly supported me in my efforts to build memories for our kids that were influenced by memories of my childhood.

TABLE OF CONTENTS

Acknowledgments	6
Foreword	8
Introduction	11
Chapter 1: THE HOLLOW TREE	15
Chapter 2: THE TRUCK	20
Chapter 3: WHY SHEEP?	27
Chapter 4: THE BB GUN	32
Chapter 5: A GIANT SHADOW	37
Chapter 6: TRIKES, BIKES, AND TOTE GOTES	42
Chapter 7: HOSKINS LUMBER CO.	46
Chapter 8: TRAINS	55
Chapter 9: BOARDS AND NAILS, HAMMERS AND SAWS	59
Chapter 10: PLACES NEED NAMES	66
Chapter 11: FAMILY HERITAGE	72
Chapter 12: TINY OUR DOG, WILD BEASTS, AND BURIED TREASURE	76

Chapter 13: OUR TELEVISION
                HEROES   85
Chapter 14: THE '49 PLYMOUTH   91
Chapter 15: BAND OF BROTHERS   97
Chapter 16: HAPPY TRAILS   102
About the Author   106
Moser Gang Gallery   109

ACKNOWLEDGMENTS

The highest thanks and praise go to my Heavenly Father, for it is God who made little children and created the playground for them to have adventures and let their imaginations come to life.

And to my Lord Jesus, for it was him who said, "Let the little children come to me, and do not hinder them, for the kingdom of God belongs to such as these."

Heartfelt thanks to my wife, Trish, who inspired me to write this book and kindly encouraged me through the whole process. She spent many hours listening to my stories, typing, proofreading, and editing to turn the dream of this book into reality.

Special thanks to my daughter, Sayde, who combined her professional resources and talents and heart to bring this book to publication.

Great gratitude to Sheila Hitchcock for her beautiful pen and ink drawing of the Good Seed Ranch home, included at the end of this book.

I am grateful for my parents, Linn and Roberta Moser. My father's life inspired countless Moser Gang adventures and he also rescued us from many of them. He was an honorary member of the gang. My mother spent many years raising all five of us and truly was the "Den Mother" of the Moser Gang.

FOREWORD

BY SAYDE WALKER

As long as I can remember my dad has been telling stories.

Sometimes the stories came in the form of Hardy Boys books read aloud at night after dinner, his love for theatrics (and making us laugh) bringing the different characters to life.

Other stories he would make up on the fly. In particular I remember there was a stuffed bear that used to ride on the dashboard of his pickup truck and go on wild adventures during the day while dad was at work. Dad would tell us about these adventures - as told to him by the bear - during dinner.

Dad also had stories about his childhood, and

those were always some of my favorites. We'd laugh until we were crying listening to him tell the tale of he and his brother in the dead of night in their pajamas on all fours pretending to be a truck, making horn honking noises with their mouths to scare all the cows lurking on the road in front of them. Or the time he searched for hours for something called "elbow grease." We heard stories about hitting a skunk with his car on his way to pick up a date, and driving a car across a frozen pond.

I remember one of these stories my dad had used as a writing assignment in 7th grade. This particular story was about the time his younger brother was dropped inside a hollowed-out tree trunk. It was so good I convinced him to publish it - and I convinced the newspaper where I was interning to print it.

I can't think of another story we ever ran that got more attention than dad's memorable tale of accidentally trapping his brother in a tree trunk. Everyone who read it loved it! Why? Because it was relatable. It was funny. It was nostalgic. The joy my dad felt while he wrote down his story transferred to everyone who read it.

When my siblings and I were little our

dad was a pastor. Which makes sense, when you think about it, because the Bible is full of stories. Stories of triumph. Stories of tragedy. Stories of overcoming all odds. Stories about everyday people turned heroes. Stories of what it looks like to walk out on faith. Stories that reveal the possibility of miracles. Even Jesus used parables to help teach his followers about the goodness of God. These stories show us the heart of God.

There are probably a million different ways God could have revealed himself to us, but He chose to do it in stories. Because stories are powerful. Stories can heal. They can bring us together. They can make us laugh, and make us cry. They can connect us to one another and make us ponder something bigger. Stories help answer questions. Above all they can bring us joy, and they show us how much God loves us. That is the purpose of stories.

This book is a compilation of dad's stories - many of them centered around him and his brothers. I've known most of these stories my entire life and I'm so excited for you to read them. May they bring you great joy, and may they inspire you to tell your own stories.

INTRODUCTION

The adventures you are about to embark on are some of my most favorite stories to recall. What you are about to read, to the best of my 72-year-old recall, is true. Now, I love a good story and if you can use your imagination like we did when we were kids, you may just find these stories will come alive like they did for us in real time.

Imagine this: Five young boys (ages six-ish to ten-ish), 500 acres to explore and conquer, materials to build stuff, and a backdrop in time of the late 1950's to early 1960's.

The first chapter of this story was written when I was in the seventh grade and had to write an essay about a true event that had happened while growing up. When I turned in my assignment, I got an "F" because my teacher did not believe it was a true experience.

When I brought the failing grade home to my mom she went through that change from the nice, loving mommy to the fighting momma bear who just realized one of her cute little cubs had been thrown under the bus! She proceeded to find pictures to prove the story and charged into the teacher's classroom to redeem her son's integrity. Wow... never had so much fun getting an "A" on a paper!

The second chapter of the Moser Gang's escapades, "The Truck," was written about 12 years ago in response to "The Hollow Tree" story being published in a newspaper run by one of my daughters. One of my nieces thought I should put more of the Moser Gang stories of our childhood to paper, so that led to its writing.

Everything following describes the adventures of these five boys as they once again came alive in my memory and ended up in this book. Even I find it difficult to believe that what you are about to read actually happened many, many years ago. I have come to believe that young children learning about life and using their God-given imaginations, live in a time frame that is most precious. So much transformation in life that follows emerges from that cocoon we call "childhood."

CHAPTER 1.

THE HOLLOW TREE

The five of us sat on the front porch, trying to decide what the basic plan of action would be that day. The five—my two brothers, two cousins and I—made up a party that went by the title of the Moser Gang. This was a unanimous choice, mainly because we were all Mosers, and the 'gang' part added what we thought was a tough sound.

That summer, like the many that had preceded it, we would roam around the hills and do everything from shooting at each other with BB guns to swimming in the nude at midnight.

As the summers went by and we grew older we did more and more things to get us into trouble. Everything we did was for fun and adventure, and though many times things got out of hand, we always seemed to end up okay. Many of our adventures have quite a story behind them, a lot of fun and usually contain a lesson we learned the hard way.

One of our little escapades that happened one summer revolves around something many people won't swallow until they see it. Then when they do see it and hear how it came about, well, they still don't believe it. This something I am talking about is a tree—a gigantic tree with a door cut in the side. On the inside there is a built-in ladder that allows a small person to climb up inside the tree.

The first question anybody might ask is, "Whatever made you decide to put a door in the side of a tree?" Well, one thing led to another and, like nearly all things we did, there is a story behind it.

We first found the tree when we were hunting for an arrow we had lost while shooting at our neighbor's cows, which somehow had wandered onto our place. The tree stood out because of its size and because it had a hole in it about ten feet up on one side.

CHAPTER ONE

My older brother, the leader at that time, wondered what was on the inside of the tree. We, or should I say my little brother, found out for him. He was the smallest one of our gang and also the most gullible.

Backtracking a little bit to the part where I said my older brother was at that time the leader of the gang... The head of our gang was our commander-in-chief and we called him Captain. He was chosen for his outstanding ability and unlimited bravery. For example, my cousin had been the leader once because he let us roll him down a hill in an oil drum. My older brother was now the leader because his maple pole with a nail in the end was the only one that stuck hard enough to stay in one of our neighbor's cows.

Now that our process of election is explained, let's get back to my story.

We told my little brother he could be the captain of our gang and be the big man if he would crawl down that hole and see what the scoop was. Well, he didn't exactly want all the responsibility that bad and was content with being the little man of the gang. But, well, we thought differently. So, we boosted him up to the hole and down he went.

After we had gotten him to quit screaming and looked the situation over, we decided we were in a fix. My older brother suggested we go back to the house and get ropes and ladders and do it like the rescue guys and firemen. But, my older cousin, who we nearly killed doing things that way, disagreed completely.

To explain his reason, we will have to go back about a summer or two. We find us in the process of building a fort around a clump of trees. My older cousin, who claimed he was looking out for wild animals (such as our dog or perhaps some of our very tame donkeys), fell out of the tree.

We did not see it happen and did not see his head hit a branch on the way down, so we naturally didn't think he was hurt. We kids had always been terrific fakers, a habit which can prove to be dangerous, and this is one lesson we learned the hard way.

We ran over to him the instant he fell and told him to get off all the branches we had just piled up. Well, he moaned a lot and screwed up his face and we thought he was doing one of his better jobs of faking!

CHAPTER ONE

The rest of us decided to go along with his act so we built a boy scout type emergency stretcher, which outweighed the five of us put together, and tried to pack him home. That didn't work and about then he started to vomit, so we had to have an easier and quicker way to get him home. We went a little ways with him strung over a bicycle but he really started getting sick and we were getting scared so we went and got our dads. With the help of our parents, we got him home and then to the hospital. Heck, he only had a severe concussion.

So, back to the tree story... We did not use the ropes and ladders, but instead we went about it like civilized boys. We got a keyhole saw, which is a saw with about a ten-inch blade, and an old drill and we proceeded to get my little brother out of the tree. The drill was used to make a hole on the side of the tree so the saw could fit into the hole.

Now, have you ever tried to cut a square door in the side of a tree about five inches thick with a little bitty saw? Well, it only took us about half a day to do it and by this time my little brother was scared something horrible. But we got him out and like everything we did, "all's well that ends well."

CHAPTER 2.

THE TRUCK

The Moser Gang Rides Again

My older brother was only two years older than me but man, oh man, could he come up with great ideas. I know it's because he had two more years to think about stuff but bigger than that, he was Captain of the Moser Gang, so he had to have great ideas. Because our dads worked in a sawmill, my two brothers and two cousins and I (who made up the Moser Gang) had access to a lot of boards and nails, and you can build just about anything with that combination.

One winter we got five or six inches of snow, so my big brother got the vision for a wooden sled

CHAPTER TWO

that could hold the whole gang. Sadly, by the time we got done nailing it together, the snow had long past melted away and the sled sat in a field next to our house for years like a used piece of farm equipment.

As Captain of the Moser Gang, he guided his faithful followers in the building of many an A-frame cabin, rope-steering carts, and could he ever build a great wooden gun. You take a 1x6 piece of lumber, drill a hole for a trigger, make a couple of cuts for a barrel and a stock and you've got yourself a rifle. Saunders, Kirby and Little John, our heroes from the television show Combat, had nothing on us as we fought many a battle in the back woods.

Then there was the wooden airplane. My brother was pretty crestfallen when Dad told him it really wouldn't fly, but at least he told him before we had to build the wings.

Dad was a very important part of our many projects and really, if he had not been so old, he probably could have been a part of the gang. There was many a meeting at the dinner table with Dad drawing on a napkin how to build something, or having the wisdom to tell us our

THE MOSER GANG

latest project would never work.

My little brother and I mostly just listened because I think Dad had already figured out that his oldest boy had all the fixer and builder type brains in the family. Ever since I could remember, when I saw a flashlight, I just turned it on to see if any light came out. But my brother would take a flashlight, or a camera, or a Tonka truck, or whatever, and take it completely apart. Then he'd be able to put it back together again! And most of the time, it would work just like before with hardly ever any parts left over.

I tried one time to go it on my own and I built a rope steering cart. Did it just like I'd seen my brother do it, but it just wouldn't roll freely down the hill. When my dad returned home from deer hunting with his buddies, I asked him to help me get my cart fixed. One of the guys with him told me all I needed was "elbow grease." So, without waiting for any further information, I raced over to the sawmill to search the oil shed for some "elbow grease." When I returned empty handed, Dad and his friends explained this mysterious grease to me. I think Dad must have known why I never got a promotion in the Moser Gang.

This story is supposed to be about the truck,

CHAPTER TWO

so I suppose I better get to telling it. Up behind our house, past our barn, two old trucks and a bulldozer had been put to rest. They belonged to my grandpa and had to be really old because he was the oldest person that I knew. These old machines of the past were like giant toys, just

"... an actually running, moving, gas burning 1932 truck that could move us down any road we could find."

waiting for us kids to bring them back to life. Once we got the mice chased out of the cabs, we were ready to haul logs and lumber and build roads to places known only to our imaginations.

These adventures in heavy equipment operation were usually pretty harmless, except for one time when we found an extra truck tire and wondered if we could get it to roll down the slope. Oh yeah, that tire not only rolled, but after it gained speed, it went airborne a couple of times as it bounced and flew to the bottom of the draw. What was a couple of seconds of whooping, hollering and laughing turned into hours of sweating, grunting and regret as Dad made us roll that truck tire all the way back to where we found it.

After a couple of years of "make believe" truck driving, my older brother once again had one of those brainstorms. Now by this time he had reached the old age of twelve, so it was probably time to move past the pretend stuff. He actually got one of those old trucks running. Don't really know how he did because I was still trying to figure out "elbow grease."

We quickly moved way past wooden sleds, airplanes and guns, to five boys and an internal combustion engine! The Mickey Mouse Club,

CHAPTER TWO

Leave it to Beaver and My Three Sons never had what we did... an actually running, moving, gas burning 1932 truck that could move us down any road we could find.

There had been a wooden bed on the back of the truck that we removed and replaced with a seat on a board so a couple of us could ride on the back since there was only room for three of us to ride in the cab. We never got too far down the road without either the brakes locking up or the gas line getting plugged. One of my cousins and my brother would grab the wrenches when the gas line plugged, and my other cousin and I had the very important job of blowing on the gas line until the glob blew back into the tank. Then we had to suck on the line until the gas flowed out. After a day of this kind of driving, I usually had a bellyache and a taste in my mouth that no amount of peanut butter sandwiches could get rid of.

The most memorable run in that old truck was riding shotgun with my brothers in the cab, picking up gears and speed as we raced to the bottom of a rock quarry behind our house.

There was an enormous puddle of water dead ahead. By the look in my brother's eyes, I realized we were about to part those waters like Moses did the Red Sea. I had been told my whole life that when you faced death, your life passed before your eyes. I don't think we were facing death or anything like that, but the one thing that flashed before all our eyes was that the old '32 truck didn't really have any floorboards.

That wave of water came up through that cab like a backwards Niagara Falls and our screaming and laughing echoed off the rock walls of that quarry for miles and miles…

Wow! What a glorious day! Three boys all water baptized in the cab of a '32 Ford truck!

CHAPTER 3.

WHY SHEEP?

My dad loved animals. At least I know he loved dogs, donkeys and... sheep. We had about 40 sheep that my dad raised on a hundred-acre piece of our property. I think it's interesting that when I look back on those memories of raising sheep, I realize we never ate lamb. Never even considered eating them. Now, my wife can prepare lamb that is as good and fine tasting to the meat-eating side of my palate as any meat I've ever had. But we raised the sheep for wool and, I suppose, to sell to that part of the population that actually enjoyed eating mutton.

THE MOSER GANG

Once a year we would round them up and shear them to remove the wool. Also, at this time my dad would take the young male sheep and stretch a rubber washer over their male parts and that would cause the most important parts of any male anatomy to fall off. Just writing about this causes me a discomfort that makes me want to move along with this story. I'm thinking this is one big reason why I never wanted to be a sheep farmer.

One of my least favorite activities that is a part of this "sheep shearing" was a job us boys had to perform. Once the sheep shearing man had shaved all the wool off the sheep, my dad would bundle it up and hoist it into a long gunny sack. The sack hung in a wooden frame and would hold a whole bunch of bundles of wool.

Now, the role of one of us boys (I don't remember my older brother ever having to do it but I'm thinking he preceded me in this very unpleasant task) was to be let down inside the gunny sack to tamp down the wool. Yes, you have the correct mind picture: a burlap gunny

CHAPTER THREE

sack with a human little boy inside who would look up to see the wool bundle as it was stuffed down on top of him. Then he would push it down until he could get on top of it and tamp it down with his feet.

I don't know how many of you have ever seen, felt or sadly tasted the rear end of a sheep's backside. All sorts of "debris" clinging to that part of a sheep's anatomy would smear all over your face. Each bundle brought you closer to the surface where the sun actually did shine, and the air did not have a distinct odor.

As I write this chapter, I am reminded of a couple of other sheep stories. I remember one time my mom and dad and my two brothers were herding the sheep into the corral. My little brother could not have been but four or five years old and one ram (with huge horns!) decided that the weakest link in this human fence was my little brother. Now, we have all probably seen sheep walk, and maybe on occasion jog, but did you know they can also jump? I recall the look on my brother's face and in his eyes as that ram went airborne and literally jumped over him, made a four-point landing on the other side and was gone! As young men we never cussed or used the Lord's name in vain, but I bet on the inside he was saying, "What the hell?!"

Another incident that happened was on a Saturday morning when my dad and us boys were gathered to go find the sheep and drive them to the barn. Only on that day my dad told us to just wait, that he had a friend coming to help. The help that his friend brought was of the four-footed kind that barks. This hero dog was given a command, and it took off with a mission! After waiting for what seemed like an eternity (young people's time clocks move a lot faster than adults') we looked out to see the sheep coming single file with the hero dog bringing up the rear. (I feel like this might have been the last year we raised sheep because I would have other dog stories if we'd ever had to corral them again.) The dog was instantly deserving of a life-long membership in the Moser Gang.

CHAPTER THREE

I started this sheep story with how my dad loved those sheep. He could call them, and they knew his voice and would come to the barn. I think they loved him, too. I tried on numerous occasions to get them to answer my voice and they paid me no attention whatsoever. They knew my dad would feed them, shelter them and as their shepherd, take care of them. My dad was pretty awesome; he could take care of mom and us and the sheep, too!

CHAPTER 4.

THE BB GUN

Different physical objects have unique effects on young boys: their first pocketknife, their first bicycle, their first fishing pole. But I don't believe anything equals that of my very first BB gun. Getting a BB gun is like a rite of passage for a boy. No longer a life of Mattel toy six-shooters or wooden guns that you had to pretend actually fired a bullet, but a "real" loading of a round projectile into a gun that you could actually aim and hit something.

Before I go any further I must be diligent to talk about gun safety. We all know that with a BB gun you could put your eye out. Having

CHAPTER FOUR

quoted that famous line, I almost did put my eye out. Twice, but only once with a BB gun. This recollection, like others to follow, is one of the more stupid ones. (You have to be honest enough to tell some stupid moments so your readers realize that all the other funny and entertaining episodes did not happen in a vacuum.) Yes, there were times when we checked our brains at the door.

Nearly going blind in one eye was due to thinking it would be cool to stick the little round stick-on caps that were made to put in your cap gun, on a cement floor and then fire your BB gun straight down on them to set off the cap. The BB ricocheted back up and hit me on the left side of my nose next to my left eye. Place your finger up there and you can see how close I came to wearing an eye patch. I would put my finger up there but it still hurts to touch it.

Ok, back to some gun safety stuff. My dad was a gun lover and sportsman and there were guns all over our house. We were informed on how to respect them and then disciplined in

THE MOSER GANG

how to hold them, how to check to see if they were loaded, how to load them, and then how to shoot them in the safest way a gun-owning father could teach his boys.

But I really believe I would be irresponsible as a storyteller if I did not paint a little better portrait of my dad. My dad was awesome! So many of our Moser Gang adventures started from seeds that he planted in our imaginations. Those seeds were either from escapades he and his brother did as young boys or by what I believe were adventures that he never got to do but wanted to see the fruit of those ideas brought to harvest by us.

As an example, let's continue on with the topic of guns, maybe minus some of the protocol for how they should be used. One Christmas we all got either a Mattel shell-shooting pistol or rifle. These toy gun replicas were amazing. Not only did they look like the real thing, but they actually shot plastic bullets out of the barrel. So, you could set up a target like a soda

CHAPTER FOUR

can and aim, let your breath out, squeeze the trigger and... bull's eye!

Now, on that particular Christmas morning there weren't any soda cans sitting around so Dad proceeded to show off his marksmanship by pulling down the sights on my mom's ornaments hanging on the tree. Then, just like a carnival shooting gallery, one by one the ornaments exploded as he shot them! Nothing quite like four young boys (one not so young) having a whoop and holler at my mom's expense!

There are more gun stories to come because so many of the Moser Gang tales have strings that attach to guns. You just didn't explore and conquer 500 acres of wilderness without weapons to be used to defend us against "who knows what" out there!

I want to close this chapter by sharing about the importance of a gift. When it's getting close to your eighth or ninth birthday and you have a brother two years older and you remember what he got for that "rite of passage" birthday, you start to get excited.

THE MOSER GANG

My mom was a wonderful woman and I know she loved us boys, but this was a gift that really needed to come from our dad. I mean, I'm not showing up for a Moser Gang outing showing off my new sweater that my mom got for my birthday. No way! I showed up with a German made, single-shot BB gun rifle that my dad ordered from his favorite sporting goods store. Nothing like a gift from a father you know so loves you.

CHAPTER 5.

A GIANT SHADOW

A lot of growing up and learning the right paths to go down happens by taking some wrong roads first. Not all the Moser Gang's adventures ended with the proper outcomes but almost always a lesson was learned.

We had entered a phase when we thought we were clever practical jokers. But oftentimes the people we were unexpectedly playing pranks on thought they were not funny, and it took some adult observations to straighten out the future of five clueless boys.

Like I said previously, the Moser Gang consisted of my two brothers (one two years older and one two years younger than me) and my two cousins (one of which was my age and another one my older brother's age). Our dads and our grandpa, "Papa," had a family business that was one of the many local sawmills in the area.

The sawmill was our playground, which I will go into more detail about in a later chapter. On this occasion we were playing pranks on some of the crew that worked there. I am sure it was only because they worked for our parents that they put up with our juvenile shenanigans.

My older brother, Captain (he still holds that title and I still often refer to him that way), had an ongoing fascination with electricity which was woven into many of our adventures. As you could guess, this led to some "shocking" results.

One of his ideas for a stunt was to hook up an electric fence box to one of the crew member's cars so that when he touched the door handle, he would be greeted with a shock. Thankfully we were able to deny all accountability because we could not get the desired outcome. I believe it was a grounding problem. Now, my escapade on the other hand, ended in a lesson learned.

CHAPTER FIVE

There I was, squatting down at the rear wheel of another crew member's pickup truck. I glanced at my two scouts, a brother and a cousin who I think were daydreaming about lunch instead of keeping their eyes peeled as I risked my life to pull off this mission. I slowly removed the cap from the tire stem and inserted the nail to release the air from the tire. All systems were go... the air hissed out.

Suddenly, there was a change in the outside atmosphere. Where I once had sun beating down on my face was now a shadow—a very, very large shadow. It was a shadow that carried a presence of danger, a presence that felt like this was not going to end well. Papa was a big man. He had hands the size of baseball gloves and they were hard and calloused from blacksmith work. Thankfully he was a man of very few words. He picked me up by the scruff of my shirt. No, I mean he literally picked me up, legs dangling off the ground, and told me to go to the shop, get a hand pump and pump that tire back up. "Yes, sir," I said and ran to the shop wondering what the heck happened to my two lookouts.

THE MOSER GANG

Have you ever tried to pump up a tire with a manual tire pump while it was still holding the weight of the truck? Let's just say it took about as long as it did for us to roll the truck tire back up from the canyon we sent it into. You know, there could be a lesson about the Moser Gang getting involved with tires.

But I think the real lesson here is about my Papa or any other good grandparent. First of all, they are so old they have to be the smartest people alive. Papa wore bib overalls, rolled his own cigarettes, and would give us a shot of whiskey in warm water if we had a cold or sore throat.

A fond memory is spending the evening at Papa's and Nana's house, eating the best ever fried chicken and watching Papa take white bread and dip it into a glass of milk for dessert. Then he would go to his easy chair and roll a cigarette. That was an invitation for one of us boys to get on his lap. He'd pull out a wooden match, strike it on the metal button of his bib overalls and then light his cigarette and let the

CHAPTER FIVE

match burn down to the very end. Whatever kid was blessed to be sitting on his lap would blow it out. Then as the smoke trailed up to the ceiling, we would wrap an imaginary cobweb around the match and pull on it. Magically the burnt match would break (as he secretly flicked the base of it with his thumb), and we would howl with pleasure. Then the next kid would climb up onto his lap and he'd repeat the process. Papa had to smoke a lot of cigarettes!

To this day, I miss that man. He was a man of few words but as a man of integrity, his life spoke loudly for itself.

CHAPTER 6.

TRIKES, BIKES AND TOTE GOTES

Growing up has so much to do with getting from one place to another. That's right—modes of transportation. As we all know, it starts out placing one foot in front of the other. Then your parents introduce you to your first wheeled machine, the baby stroller. I think of all the time (at least for little boys), all those hours of being pushed around in the stroller so old people could smile at you and pinch your cheeks, were times of planting seeds of future two- and four-wheel adventures.

CHAPTER SIX

This was followed by the original three-wheeler, the trike. Then possibly a wagon and then a skateboard. Our skateboards were the original, real McCoy. To make them, we started with a pair of steel roller skates, the kind you clamped to your shoes, and separated the front wheels from the back ones. Then we'd cut a board about two feet long and attach a set of wheels to each end. Then off we'd go! This was way before helmets and knee pads and elbow pads so, oh yeah, there were scrapes and bruises. Then came the bike...

When Mom and Dad decided to sell the sheep, my younger brother and I got the surprise gifts that surpassed anything up to that time in our young lives.

Mom took us to the bicycle shop in Corvallis and we each got to pick out a brand-new Schwinn Stingray bike. Lime green, high butterfly handlebars and a banana seat. Oh, my... getting put down in the gunny sack, covered with sheep poop, was now all worth it.

THE MOSER GANG

The trails that once were the pathways for the sheep were now the roads to adventure for boys and their bikes. We had plenty of old logging roads to traverse and would zip down the hill, cross over the main highway (many times without stopping since not many cars passed by back in those days) and ride around the mill yard.

I remember one day my mom loaded us and our bikes in the pickup truck and she took us to Philomath where we got to spend the whole day riding up and down the streets. City kids had the advantage over the country boys when it came to having a network of flat, level streets to ride on. They also had the best pit stop ever, Dairy Queen, where a nickel bought you an ice cream cone and fifteen cents got you a milkshake! Oh yes, the value of the dollar has changed so much. I still have my Stingray bicycle and I know it is worth more today than the price of all the sheep my dad sold.

After the bicycle, for us came what was called a Tote Gote. It was originally built as a two-wheel motorized machine to traverse the hills

CHAPTER SIX

and was used for hunting and transporting game animals. When our dad began hunting deer in eastern Oregon, he built a couple of them and soon us boys had a brand-new way to explore the great outdoors. Then came the Honda trail bikes, followed by motorcycles and then the Truck. Finally, we had the famous '49 Plymouth.

Imagine all these various ways of transporting ourselves from one place to another! Oh, but what a fun ride it's been!

CHAPTER 7.
HOSKINS LUMBER COMPANY

I feel I need to start this chapter with a disclaimer. My parents were awesome parents. They watched over us and protected us and supervised us in so many ways that I am thankful for. Having said that, you must understand the backdrop of the times. Things were so different back in that time period.

We grew up less than 200 yards from my family's sawmill. We had to ride our bikes across a state highway to get to the sawmill and once we crossed that highway, we rode around log trucks, lumber trucks, log loaders and forklifts.

CHAPTER SEVEN

Once there, we played in the sawmill, under the sawmill with moving logs, moving lumber, moving rollers, moving conveyors, and noise! So much noise! But that was our world... a world of moving machinery, moving parts, and swiftly moving adventure!

At the end of the working day, when the trucks all left and the saws all shut down and the movement ceased, there was an eerie silence. I can remember playing around the house after the mill had shut down and my dad and my uncle would be doing end-of-the-day maintenance. Something would not be working the way it was supposed to and my dad would start cussing. My mom would herd us kids into the house so our poor little ears wouldn't hear words that of course, we had heard many times before (words we possibly repeated).

My dad had a particular grouping of swear words that had a rhythm and cadence all their own. If I chose to, at this moment I could recite them word for word. I can also remember getting my mouth washed out with soap for accidentally using just a portion of my dad's poetic phrases.

There are two parts of the old-style sawmills that have been replaced over time that I believe characterize the mills of yesteryear. One was what was called a wigwam burner. It actually looked like a huge metal teepee with a conveyor belt coming from under the mill, carrying the waste wood up and into the wigwam burner to be burned. The ash had to be cleaned out every so often and was accomplished with the use of a Ford 8N tractor with a bucket. It was a very dirty job but also a very fun job. I say fun because once you reached the age of twelve, you got to drive the tractor... another rite of passage.

You started with the tractor (actually, you started with a shovel, cleaning up under the mill), moved on to a forklift, a lumber carrier, a log loader and finally, to driving a truck. All of this occurred by the time we were fifteen years old. Yes, life was a little different back then.

The other vanishing part of the old sawmills was the mill pond. The mill pond at our mill

CHAPTER SEVEN

"... Once you reached the age of twelve, you got to drive the tractor.... another rite of passage"

was basically a man-made lake that the log trucks would dump their logs into so they could be sorted and then bucked to the right length for the mill. I can still see my dad wearing his cork boots (boots with spiked soles to keep from slipping), walking on the moving logs with a pike pole in his hands to push the moving logs in the right direction. I also remember him coming home soaking wet from having fallen into the pond.

Papa had a little shack on the far side of the pond with a bucking saw and a little stove to keep warm. His job was to pull the logs up to the bucking saw and cut them to the right length. Us kids would attempt to help him, but I really think all we supplied was an entertainment factor.

One cold winter day I was being Papa's right-hand man and I speared a log with my pike pole. I could not get the pole to come loose before I pushed the log away from the dock and ended up falling headfirst into the pond. I came home that day soaking wet, covered in pond slop. But I was one step closer to being like my dad!

Following in another's footsteps is how we learn how to do this life. The footsteps we

CHAPTER SEVEN

follow determine so much of who we will be. I had the privilege of placing my little boots into the steps of some giants.

WALKIN' IN THE STEPS

(Song by Bob Moser)

Little Johnny watched his brother
Climb on the seat of the tractor
Dad was teaching him about the ground
The way the land was to be tilled
Johnny listened to what his daddy had to say
Watched him and brother drive away
He watched 'til all that he could see
Were their tracks across the field

Johnny went to bed that night
With his toy tractor held tight
Thinking about his brother and the fields he plowed today
Thought about his dad's guiding hand
As he showed his brother how to work the land
Thought how he wanted to grow up
And follow in his father's ways

Chorus:
Walkin' in the steps of my brother
In the ways of my father
That's the way I want to go, don't want to go no other
I want to do what my brother's done, walk like my father's son
In the steps of my brother, in the ways of my father

John is all grown up now, he's driving a tractor and pulling a plow
Working by his brother's side in the fields their dad did sow
He's got a family of his own
Couple of boys, they're almost grown.
And he's teaching them what his daddy taught him
So many years ago

Chorus:
Walkin' in the steps of my brother
In the ways of my father
That's the way I want to go, don't want to go no other
I want to do what my brother's done, walk like my father's son
In the steps of my brother, in the ways of my father

Put God first, son, in all you do
He'll bless the ground; He'll prosper you
Thank Him for His blessings, every single day
Jesus Christ was God's first-born son
He laid the foundation we build upon
And you can walk in his steps, son
And in your Father's ways

Chorus:
Walkin' in the steps of my Brother
In the ways of my Father
That's the way I want to go, don't want to go no other
I want to do what my Brother's done, walk like my Father's son
In the steps of my Brother, in the ways of my Father

CHAPTER 8.

TRAINS

The steam locomotive was the tip at the end of the spear that carried industry and passengers not only to the West but also to the North and South, too. Most of my generation missed the greatness of this movement but my grandfather, Papa, grew up right in the middle of it. Thus, his admiration and praise for the steam locomotive. Because of his attachment and interest, my uncle and dad also loved everything to do with trains. That found its way to the Moser Gang.

The little settlement of Hoskins was kind of a railroad hub where the train from the timber town of Valsetz in the coast mountains would pass through Hoskins to get to the Independence railhead. There was a wheelhouse or railway turntable in Hoskins that would spin the engine around to go back the way it came. So, Papa had plenty of train activity right in his backyard, so to speak.

Papa also had a love for what they called a traction engine, which was used to pull plows, run sawmills, and power threshing machines. They had giant steel wheels taller than any of us boys and we played on them and rode on them whenever Papa would fire one up. There was one special occasion when they put on an old-fashioned threshing bee in a field by his house and people traveled from all over to witness a step into the past. The local news channel put it on the nightly news, and I remember watching it later on our black and white T.V.

Papa's love for trains led him to purchase a scaled-down version of a real steam locomotive, complete with passenger cars. He, along with my dad and uncle, built nearly two miles of

CHAPTER EIGHT

track that started at the sawmill and wove up into the hills surrounding the mill. They would lay out the ties and spike the rails down using a railroad gauge to keep the right width. The Moser Gang would lend support and at times, confusion, to the project that took a couple of years to complete. On any given Sunday we would see the black smoke coming from the engine as Papa fired the boiler, and we would grab our bikes and pedal over to help him give rides to people that would stop by on their way to the coast.

Over the next half a year, the Moser Gang watched as my dad, uncle and grandpa built a modern diesel scaled locomotive that had room for one adult and one gang member to ride in the cab. Soon we got to operate it by ourselves and spent hours running up and down the tracks, pulling the passenger car with the whole gang yelling and cheering in the back.

There was something about this season of the Moser Gang that felt like it spanned three generations. Papa, Dad, my uncle, and us five all seemed to be young boys living out our dreams.

"The little settlement of Hoskins was kind of a railroad hub where the train from the timber town of Valsetz in the coast mountains would pass through."

CHAPTER 9.

BOARDS AND NAILS, HAMMERS AND SAWS

What?! How long do you want me to make this boat (or, should I say, Animal Cruise Ship)? Do you realize, God, that there are battle ships smaller than this floating zoo?

Well, we never went to my dad to see how to build something of the magnitude of Noah's Ark, but golly gee, we sure built a lot of fun structures out of wood. Probably because our parents owned a sawmill, and that sawmill made boards, and we had a tool shed with a barrel full of nails and hammers and saws. I suppose it was just a natural progression to dream it and then build it.

Captain had most of the ideas for what we nailed together, and we started small and simple and went skyward from there. Swords and spears came first and then we moved on to forts and tree houses. My cousin, the same age as me, and my older brother had an incredible ability to be able to saw a straight line with a hand saw and could drive in nails without hardly ever bending them over. The rest of us had jobs like packing the boards, holding the boards in place, and standing on the end of the boards while they were being cut. It took all of our hands and feet working together to bring our projects to completion.

Our building projects, I guess like everything in life, started out small and simple and then graduated in proportion to our abilities and imaginations. Our first forts were just sticks and brush piled up to form a perimeter where we could play army and eat peanut butter sandwiches. We later built another fort out of

CHAPTER NINE

split-rail cedar fence posts, and that was accomplished simply by laying two posts on the ground about six feet apart and then stacking two more on top of those, going the other direction. Then two more placed on top going the other way and up the building went. (If you have ever played with Lincoln Logs, you get the picture.) One log had to be set in a little to make a door and then a couple of posts were placed together to make a bunkbed.

I remember one night we decided to sleep in our fort overnight but didn't take into consideration how the wind would blow right through our structure. Dad let us stay out there just long enough for us to claim it as an adventure and then he came and rescued us.

That building project was named "Fort Broken Wing" in memory of the buzzard Captain knocked out of the sky with his Daisy BB gun. The hill it was built on still carries that name today.

A-frame cabins were our next building type, and these had doors and windows to keep the wind out. Our first one was a treehouse version that was up in a giant oak tree by our barn. It was rather small and could only accommodate

"... Our parents owned a sawmill, and that sawmill made boards.... I suppose it was just a natural progression to dream it and then build it."

CHAPTER NINE

a couple of the gang at a time, so soon we built another one over on the piece of land where the Hollow Tree had taken root. For many years this was our go-to clubhouse. Mom and Dad so loved that location that they built a house on the exact spot where our A-frame had stood.

The last A-frame my older brother designed and built was many years later overlooking a small lake my dad had made. This one was huge with a spiral staircase going up to the second story. Like I said, our building adventures just kept getting bigger and bigger!

We also used 4x4 boards to build the simplest rope-steering carts. Nail three of them together, set them on some old tricycle axles and you have a fast ride down a hill. My dad helped my older brother turn one into a really awesome firetruck. It had a little box hood with a window and a small oil barrel painted red on the back for a water tank. This was all well and good until he decided that if he had a firetruck, then he needed a fire to put out. My dad and his hunting buddies were drinking coffee and smoking cigarettes in the kitchen when we came in and told them the Fire Chief had lit a tree on fire. You know, big people can move really fast when they need to!

Once again, having these kinds of imaginations and then having the opportunity to actually do some of the things we imagined, paid off in spades later in life. Captain ended up building his own house, my older cousin built apartments, and as for me, well, I've raised a roof or two during my lifetime.

Being able to build something can put a lot of pieces called "life" together. Using the wrong materials, the wrong tools, and laying out an improper foundation can all be the hard way to learn a life lesson.

Having the imagination to see a buildable structure in your mind and then the "how" to bring it into manifestation is really a cool thing to be able to do. There is something about having the plan and making it happen that sets a fire in a young person's mind. I believe that's from the One who dreamed up the creation

CHAPTER NINE

of heaven and earth and had the brainstorm of forming, making and creating the being we call "man."

CHAPTER 10.

PLACES NEED NAMES

Most all of our adventures had a destination… either a place or a completion of a plan or project inspired by our imaginations. Many of those landing places for our escapades had names that have remained the same to this very day. I mentioned Fort Broken Wing in a previous chapter, and I want to share a number of other names attached to the areas where we roamed.

The first one that comes to mind was the road that began behind our house and climbed up to the sheep barn. We called it the "New Road." It was just steep enough that you had

CHAPTER TEN

to get a run at it with your bicycle in order to pedal to the top. Not that easy when you realize we didn't have ten-speed bikes.

That hill had just enough slope to make a ride down on a rope-steering cart a perilous adventure. To get the full image of this high-speed enactment, you need to visualize a rope-steering cart. This "race car" consisted of three 4x4 posts nailed together. A tricycle axle and wheels were nailed underneath the back end and another set was nailed on the front, held by a bolt in the middle so it could steer. A rope was attached to the left and right sides so you could try to control whichever direction you wanted to go. Usually, you were just trying to keep it on a straight course.

I feel I should include in this segment of the story a tale in which the guilty members of the Moser Gang will never be revealed because of our code of honor. Having absolved all guilty parties, I can tell you about this one time that the cart charging down the New Road ended in what I shall call a pre-designed mishap.

THE MOSER GANG

A friend from the city had come over one afternoon and having been a spectator of different gang members racing down the hill, he decided he had built up enough courage to straddle the cart and get propelled down the New Road.

While he was getting himself situated on the projectile, someone (name will never, ever be revealed), removed the bent nail from the rear axle that held the wheel on. Yes, folks, there was a crash! Can't believe I'm actually saying this, but it was a magnificent crash!

Halfway down the hill, the wheel shot off, the cart went out of control and careened off the road and flipped over into a bumper crop patch of poison oak. None of us Moser Gang kids had ever gotten poison oak, so we didn't really ever pay attention to the consequences of rolling in it. Not so with the casualty of this tragic mishap. Okay, I really should end this misadventure and share a story about another road that still retains its name.

Old dried-up bones of a cow on the side of a road were the inspiration of calling it the

CHAPTER TEN

"Dead Cow Road." Many a blue jay hunt took place on this road and when we came of age to hunt deer, many a horned critter got tagged on that section of property.

There is a memory attached to the Dead Cow Road that almost has a spooky sense to it. Not that we thought there were ghosts or goblins or anything like that because we were way too old to believe in that sort of nonsense. But because I can't remember how this adventure took seed, and all I can recall is the middle and end of it, it seems kind of eerie.

Where and when the memory starts is that Captain and I were out on the Dead Cow Road late at night in our pajamas. Now, our house is a good half mile from this road so, like I said, I just don't remember why we ended up there. But we did, and it was dark, and we suddenly realized there were animals all around us. We could not see them, but we could hear and smell them.

Now, we might have been just a little scared. Okay, you're right, we were terrified! But fear

THE MOSER GANG

not; my older brother once again lived up to his high rank of Captain and came up with a plan. He recalled how we had ridden on the tailgate of my dad's pickup truck on that very same road many times, and how Dad would honk his horn and gun the motor when the cows were blocking the road. So, on our hands and knees we proceeded to crawl up that road, making honking sounds and motor noises. Once we cleared the cow-infested area, we rose to our feet and hotfooted it all the way back to the house and the safety of our beds.

The last landmark location I want to mention bears the name of "Lone Fir." It is a hill (or mountain if you're from Kansas) that rises to the highest elevation of the property we grew up on. There was a tall fir tree that crowned this hill, thus being the namesake for that location. As young boys, this was always the destination of many a hiking adventure. As we grew older, it was always a prime deer hunting site and the place where I bagged my first deer. Today it holds a sacred atmosphere as the ashes of my

CHAPTER TEN

godfather, my grandparents, and my mom and dad are spread over the top of Lone Fir.

When I stand on that hill today, memories of all those loved ones come to the surface. There were opening day mornings of deer season when my brothers and I all gathered with my godfather, my grandfather, and my dad to discuss how that particular hunt was going to proceed. We all know life moves on and to have fond memories of places and loved ones is a blessing that makes the heart thankful.

CHAPTER 11.

FAMILY HERITAGE

Both of my parents' families came west to Oregon around the 1860's. My mom's family migrated from England and my dad's came west from Tennessee.

My recollections of both of these journeys are pretty much based on the stories we were told as young Moser Gang members. Are they true? Well, they sounded good to us back then and I've never heard anyone contradict them so they must be at least partly true.

Mom's side of the story is about two brothers that came from England to buy land in Oregon. They came in the winter or spring when the

CHAPTER ELEVEN

Willamette River had just flooded. The story goes they spent a couple days in what is now Eugene, perched up in a couple of trees to avoid the high moving water. Once they could move, they came north to buy land. One brother bought 2,000 acres around Corvallis and the other brother purchased 2,000 acres of rocky hill country located just outside of Philomath, extending to Wren. There is very little of their land left in the family today but back in the Moser Gang days up on Wren Hill, my folks raised three of the five gang members and built their home and a sawmill there.

Dad's ancestors came from Tennessee during the middle of the Civil War. My grandmother's grandfather, Samuel Franz, brought his wife and seven children on a wagon train to Oregon to avoid having to fight his own cousins in the war. When they arrived in King's Valley, Oregon, in the foothills of the Coast Range Mountains, there was only one remaining 640-acre parcel for sale. But, boy oh boy, did it come with a bonus. Not only did they end up with acreage with a

THE MOSER GANG

river flowing through it but also a water-wheel sawmill and... wait for it... here it comes... their very own Army fort!!

Fort Hoskins was a Union Army fort that had been disbanded by the government so the Union soldiers could return and fight for the North. Samuel Franz and his family lived in the fort's medical building until they built their home. That two-story house is still standing today on the Fort Hoskins property.

Papa, my grandpa on my dad's side, loved two things—sawmills and trains. He, along with two sons, started Hoskins Lumber Company right after World War II. The mill started out in Hoskins and then in the early fifties was moved to the top of Wren Hill to be closer to the railhead in Philomath. Every member of the Moser Gang contributed to making boards out of logs there.

Nana, my grandma on my dad's side, was the true matriarch of not just the Moser Gang but the whole family, kit and kaboodle. She had a gentle and quiet spirit that had been through

CHAPTER ELEVEN

two world wars and the Great Depression. She had a garden that was a pick-and-eat smorgasbord of berries, green peas and tomatoes, plus every type of pepper, onion, corn, cabbage, potatoes and lettuce. One of my most favorite meals to this day was her fried chicken, coleslaw, mashed potatoes, corn on the cob and green beans.

I am thankful that before she passed away at 103 years old, I became a Christian and had the privilege along with my family to be able to pray for her. I say this because I know that lady prayed for me and the rest of my Moser Gang compadres.

CHAPTER 12.

TINY OUR DOG, WILD BEASTS, AND BURIED TREASURE

When I began raising my own family, I asked my dad how he thought it was proper parenting to let your kids roam the hills all day long without any supervision. His answer was truthful, to the point and, I guess, made total sense to him. We had the dog with us!

We had a couple of different dogs growing up but the one that was a constant companion to the Moser Gang was a trained farm work dog named "Tiny." She was so smart. In all honesty,

CHAPTER TWELVE

she was a lot smarter than the five little guys she was entrusted to watch over.

When Tiny was brought into our family, we didn't have sheep anymore or any other animals for her to herd or watch guard over. So, she rose to the command position to always be there between "her" little boys and any type of danger.

She had a complete understanding of the most important English words: sit, stay, and sic 'em. The latter word was our favorite because you could give her that command and she went after whatever you pointed at. Every squirrel, rabbit and cow feared that word and would run for their lives if Tiny received that command. By the end of the summer, poor Tiny would be so covered with burrs from running and herding, we would have to have her sheared.

Now, before I get into more tales of wild beasts, I need to digress and explain some of the essential information about things that many times were necessary for a Tiny/Moser Gang adventure.

THE MOSER GANG

First, let's dive into the need for food and water when embarking on an all-day excursion in hundreds of acres of uncharted wilderness. There, of course, is only one ration that is required on a hot summer day hike and that is a peanut butter sandwich. Sometimes jam, usually not. As good as that sandwich was, it could never be compared to Nana Moser's slice of white bread, covered with butter and folded over. There is no cook-show chef that can put anything together to compare with that little boy tummy delight.

Of course, water was critical when living off peanut butter sandwiches. We all had our Army surplus canteens and on one fateful hiking trip, Captain had put lemonade in a big canteen someone had given him. Don't know what caused it but the lemonade turned rotten inside that canteen and our commanding officer got just slightly sick. I think we went forward with our mission that day... it took more than a little throwing up to stop our squad of explorers.

CHAPTER TWELVE

Another thing we had to do to prepare for an excursion was to be issued weaponry. Now, sometimes it was just a pocketknife. (Probably should never use the words, "just a pocketknife.") From a young boy to a grown man, there are not many things that define him like his pocketknife. Our knives were the jackknife variety that usually had one to three blades that folded into the handle. There was the Boy Scout version that had a knife and a spoon hooked in there somehow but when your lunch is a peanut butter sandwich you really don't need that kind of a tool. It wasn't until years later when we started hunting deer that we carried skinning knives. Not many things can transform a young boy's image like a hunting knife in a scabbard hanging on your belt.

On some treks we would cut maple shoots that grew everywhere and we'd either skin the bark off them or take our knives out and cut rings for throwing handles. Next, we would take them over to the shop at the mill, drive a nail in the ends, and put them on the grinder to sharpen the tips to a point. Then we had spears! I would never repeat this under oath, and the rest of the gang will take this information to their graves, but one time (the only time) my older brother reclaimed his title of Captain of the Moser Gang by having his perfectly thrown spear actually hit a cow and stick for a moment. Now, having told you that, I suppose it could've just been a rumor.

We would cover a lot of ground searching for blue jays and crows, but I don't ever remember coming home with anything to cook over the campfire. There was this one time though, we were all spread out in the grass on the hill in a tactical position where we could watch the buzzards' shadows. Thinking we might be their next meal, they would circle us, getting closer and lower, spying out their prey. We could tell by the size of their shadows when they were close. Then we rolled over and opened fire with our BB guns. The Captain was armed with his Daisy 200-shot lever action gun and we could see the BBs charging upward, shining in the

CHAPTER TWELVE

sun as they arced toward the flying monsters. And if we all hadn't witnessed what took place next, no one would have believed our tale. A "super BB" struck one of the buzzards and he spiraled down like a gut shot airplane and nose dived into the hillside. What?! We all looked at each other like we had witnessed the crash landing of a UFO. As fast as our short little legs could carry us, we raced toward the fallen beast. But then the big bird shook off the impact of the projectile, bounced a couple of times and flapped its wings back skyward. That was a tale that would sprout its own wings and fly into infamy.

Logging roads, jeep paths and sheep trails zigzagged the hills through meadows and canyons, and we traversed them on foot, bicycles and Tote Gotes (those motorized two-wheelers that our dad built), and later, Willys Jeeps.

One such trail would take us all the way to the river where we spent one summer moving rocks in the river to build a dam that raised the water level enough to have a swimming hole.

THE MOSER GANG

We then took some empty oil drums and slashed them together to make a raft so we could travel up the river. It wasn't the Mississippi River, but we sure did a great impression of Huck Finn.

At this point in the river there was a railroad trestle for the train that ran between the valley and the coast. We would climb up into

"The noise and the vibration of the train ... as it passed directly over our heads could barely drown out our screams of joy and excitement!"

CHAPTER TWELVE

the inside structure of the trestle and wait for the train. The noise and the vibration of the train and all the railroad cars as they passed directly over our heads could barely drown out our screams of joy and excitement!

Back to the sheep trails… While navigating some of those trails, every once in a while we would encounter the "Abominable Sheep." When my family ceased to be sheep farmers and sold our herd, a couple of the sheep missed the bus. I am sure one of them was the one that decided to high jump over my little brother in a previous chapter. Over the years, those few stragglers kept getting bigger and bigger as their wool grew and grew until they inflated to the size of small legless white elephants minus the trunks. We never got close enough to land a spear or a sling shot, and for all I know, they are still roaming the hills.

Probably the most intense drama that occupied a good portion of our exploits was the time spent looking for buried treasure. No, not from pirates because we were too far from the ocean but something just as compelling… a heist from a bank robbery! As best as I can remember, my grandpa and my dad whetted our primal appetites for this adventure. (That or they knew how to keep us close to home and more or less out of trouble.) The Philomath bank had been robbed and the outlaws were caught near the small community of Wren. We just happened to live on Wren Hill, so we were close to where the bank robbers lost their freedom. It was also where they lost the stolen loot which was never recovered. We hiked up and down hills, looked under rocks and logs and into cracks in the ground. Truth be told, it would have been why we dropped the boy with the red boots down into the hollow tree. As you've surely figured out, since we didn't all go out and buy brand new bikes and BB guns, we never discovered the hidden location of the bounty.

My summary of this rather long chapter is once again the wonderful beauty of the imaginations of youngsters. Didn't have video games or virtual reality headsets. We didn't need them. We had our imaginations!

CHAPTER 13.

OUR TELEVISION HEROES

Rabbit ears sitting on top of the old black and white T.V. were there to bring in two television stations. For the Moser Gang, that was just enough action by our heroes to produce hours upon hours of simulated adventures.

A show called Rescue Eight was one of our favorites. It was a series about two men who worked for the L.A. Fire Department, rescuing folks from disasters like collapsed buildings, car accidents and anything else involving ropes and crow bars. We would tie ropes to our belts and hang ourselves from tree limbs and usually end up having to rescue each other.

THE MOSER GANG

Twelve O'Clock High was another favorite and our dad got involved and took this T.V. series to a whole different level. One day he went to the sawmill shop with an old oval coffee table of my mom's and came home with the cockpit of a B-29 bomber. He had built two retractable steering wheels mounted to the coffee table so when you stood it on its side and put two chairs in front of it you were in the cockpit of the bomber. He then covered every available space with buttons and switches and gauges left over from mill stuff. If that wasn't cool enough, he took a small table and mounted a periscope we had bought at the GI Army surplus store. He painted crosshairs on the lens, and we would put our little toy cars under it so when you looked into one end of the periscope, it looked like you were seeing those tiny vehicles below you. That was the position the bombardier had on the B-29 bomber.

Our favorite weekly show and the one we spent the most time re-enacting was another World War II show called Combat. For this one

CHAPTER THIRTEEN

we made wooden M1 Garand rifles and tommy guns. The rest of our gear my dad bought at the Army surplus store and outfitted us with an army belt with ammo pouches, canteens and folding shovels. The acreage that we roamed became Germany and France, and the barn and sawmill became towns that we had to set free from German occupation.

Something that still today is difficult to process is how my dad had so many friends that actually in real life had been those soldiers and pilots. He also had friends that never came home, that paid the highest sacrifice anyone could offer—their lives for someone else. There was a blanket of silence over that generation. I don't think they ever talked about it with their wives, family or each other. We kids imitated our T.V. heroes, but in reality, we lived with, worked with and learned from real-time heroes.

Television shows back in the 50's and 60's usually ended with a moral or life lesson. The Donna Reed Show, Leave it to Beaver, My Three Sons, Father Knows Best, and even Bonanza, left you with something to think about.

THE MOSER GANG

Growing up and in the present time, we have heroes all around us. The moms and dads, teachers and coaches, military patriots and others can affect and change the direction of our lives. Take a look around. And of course, the man that started shaking things up a couple thousand years ago and is still doing it today—Jesus, the Son of God—is the absolute greatest living hero of all time.

HEROES

(Song by Bob Moser)

I remember when I was just a kid
Pretending to be our heroes is what we did
To wear a cape or a white hat were the games we used to play
In the comic books we would find
They came to life in our minds
And on Saturday morning T.V. we'd watch them save the day

Chorus:
They would ride out on the double
Find the lost, hurting and in trouble
Rescue them from evil, help them find their way
Give them hope and courage for a new day
Climb in the saddle and ride away
Into the sunset—they were our heroes

On my t-shirt I painted a giant "S"
My cape was a towel tied around my neck
And there was no strength like the power of Superman
Or I was out west staring down danger
Riding shotgun with the Texas Rangers
Riding tall in the saddle, guns blazing in my hands

THE MOSER GANG

Chorus:
And we'd ride out on the double
Find the lost, hurting and in trouble
Rescue them from evil, help them find their way
Give them hope and courage for a new day
Climb in the saddle and ride away
Into the sunset—we were the heroes

Then I grew up and I found
There were real live heroes all around
Those willing to give their all
To make the ultimate sacrifice
Those with courage to face the lions
Poised on either side
Those willing to say yes
Those willing to give their life

Then I realized down through the ages
The greatest heroes are on the Bible pages
And the greatest of them all
Is our Lord Jesus Christ
He gave his life to conquer sin
Now we can be born again
And we go out and speak his words of life

Chorus:
We ride out on the double
Find the lost, hurting and in trouble
Rescue them from evil, help them find their way
Give them hope and courage for a new day
Lead them to Jesus who is the Way
Get them saved—by the greatest hero

CHAPTER 14.

THE '49 PLYMOUTH

When you are growing up there are so many modes of transportation you graduate through before you get to the automobile. Not going to count the baby carriage because I don't think any of us remember those free, no-effort-involved trips to the park, the store or other parts of the New World. But think about what followed: tricycles, roller skates, scooters, skateboards, bicycles, rope steering carts, Tote Gotes, motorcycles, and then... an internal combustion engine, four tires and a steering wheel.

Now, we actually started with the '32 Ford farm truck. This vehicle of transportation was introduced in the chapter, "The Truck." It was all good, except only a few Moser Gang members got to actually ride in the cab, and breakdowns occurred way too often. Also, I should reveal that, to the best of my memory, only the Captain got to be behind the wheel. So, let's move our ages down the timeline a little bit and introduce the '49 Plymouth. Every boy remembers his first car, and this was our first "Gang Mobile."

I'll get right back to this hot rod, but I want to insert a description of my own personal "first car." I do this, not to agonize classic car collectors, but to once again portray the way life was back in the early sixties.

I think I was probably about fourteen years old and starting to dream about cars. My dad decided I needed a "project" car. So, we went to this guy's house that had a field that was not grazing livestock, but old cars (actually most of them were maybe ten years old). So, my dad made a deal with the guy. Only those of you reading this that lived back in those days are going to believe this. He bought a 1955 Chevy two-door hard top and paid a hefty twenty-five dollars for it. Yes, twenty-five dollars.

CHAPTER FOURTEEN

"Red Boots behind the wheel is one of my favorite '49 Plymouth stories."

Now, if that hasn't caused a true classic car person to need a heart defibrillator, my dad noticed a broken brake line, so he went back to negotiate. Instead of lowering the price, the used car dealer gave us a 1956 Chevy hard top to use for parts. The '55 got restored and my younger brother ended up actually putting some blacktop miles on it. The '56 coup, well… I mean come on, it was supposed to be for parts, though it was also restorable. Since all you car enthusiasts are already upset anyway, that Chevy ended up being used for target practice.

Okay, we better turn around quickly and get back to the star of this story—the '49 Plymouth. We came into possession of this super beast when one of the young men working at the mill decided we needed to up our game of adventure and see what kind of trouble we could get into with a real live automobile. He gave it to us for free, with only one condition. When we were done playing A.J. Foyt on the old logging roads and were finished with the car, he wanted to race it across the mill yard and roll it.

Captain decided the hot rod needed a fresh coat of paint, so we all watched as he hooked up an air sprayer and proceeded to paint our club car shiny black. Now that awe-inspiring paint job only looked cool for about one minute. You see, sometimes the grandest ideas kind of run amuck.

CHAPTER FOURTEEN

First of all, really, you don't paint out in the open, in the middle of a lumber yard. Second, you might want to make sure there is no wind. But the real deal breaker was not our fault. Well, maybe a little. We no sooner had our first, "Oh, wow, it looks awesome!" when a dude came racing his car into the yard and brought with him a dust cloud that could block out the sun. The poor ol' Plymouth went from shiny "cool, man" black to a kind of brown over black dust flake. But we recovered from the setback, and as soon as the paint was dry, we took spray cans of silver and painted numbers on the doors and trunk like real race cars had.

Red Boots behind the wheel is one of my favorite '49 Plymouth stories. He was in the front seat taking his turn at the wheel and my cousin and I were giving him driving lessons from the back seat. He had a hard time reaching the pedals so he would slide himself down by scooting off the end of the seat, gun the throttle, then pull himself up using the steering wheel to see where he was going. When he nearly sideswiped a tree, we were laughing and yelling at him. So… he turned around to see the tree he almost debarked and… "LOOK OUT!!" Off the road and over the bank we went! "It's ok! Nobody is bleeding; no broken bones." A hike back to the mill to borrow a tractor and a chain, and soon we were back on the logging road with little brother now in the back seat giving directions.

All those driving instructors that issued licenses to the Moser Gang members had no idea of where those mature driving abilities came from.

CHAPTER 15.

BAND OF BROTHERS

When my two brothers and I joined in the conquest of an idea, it took all of us to make it happen. Many times, the birthing of one of these adventures took place in the bathroom while my dad was taking his end of the workday bath. Two of us would be perched on the counter like sea gulls waiting for a handout, and the third would be on the throne. My dad's advice would be sought after for our next project, and he would either nix it before it got wings, or he would dry off his hands and ask for pencil and paper. Once his request was quickly fulfilled, he would tell us how to build the foundation first, how to square the corners, then how to gusset the walls so they wouldn't collapse.

My older brother, Captain, usually had the idea and then became the foreman for the job. Later in life he became a master mechanic and an incredible builder. I was there with my younger brother as we witnessed the beginning of a great man.

My younger brother also had a nickname that I want to take some time to explain. His most noticeable item of clothing from his early youth was not really clothing at all. It was his boots, his fire engine red boots.

Now, most little kids had a pair of rubber boots, but these had a certain aura about them that over the years actually made both him and the boots famous. There usually isn't a Moser Gang story told at family gatherings that doesn't mention the famous red boots. It is because of this that I want to elaborate a little bit.

To many, the red boots symbolized the position at the bottom of the Moser Gang hierarchy,

CHAPTER FIFTEEN

almost as the role of a flunky. This is not how I view it at all. I saw then and have grown in understanding that every person has a part to play, something that they bring to the table—an ability, an extra set of hands, a calling, or you could even say, a gift.

I have supervised a lot of men over the years and have learned by experience that your role as a leader is to match the right person to the right job. The only thing maybe more important is to always lead from the front. Or even more accurately, from the bottom up by taking the lead. From that position, you always see what is happening and when the leadership needs to get involved. At the same time you earn the respect of those working with you.

My younger brother, Mr. Red Boots, was gallant and courageous while some of us older boys had just a little yellow streak. Now you might say he was too young to know better or that he was tricked into doing something or that he wanted to prove himself as capable as we thought we were. Doesn't matter. Could be all the above.

THE MOSER GANG

I just knew he was my brother and fellow gang member. He still is today.

After our years of service ended in the Moser Gang, my older brother and I became Cub Scouts, and later, Boy Scouts. Being an officer in the Moser Gang enabled my older brother to excel at being a Boy Scout. I could hardly tie my own shoes, but he could tie any kind of knot you could imagine. He also knew how to use a compass. I mean for real, like going into the woods and not getting lost but ending up right where he was supposed to be. This is true, Scout's honor. I was with him when he did it. I don't really know how he felt but I stuck my chest out, kicked the ground, took a spit and said, "Yeah, that's my brother."

And he was also a master chef over the campfire and could build camp furniture out of maple saplings and rope. I remember one rainy morning during a weekend Boy Scout campout, my buddy and I were trying to mix up batter to make pancakes and he decided to just fill up his mess-kit fry pan to the brim with batter and stick

CHAPTER FIFTEEN

it over the fire. It ended up burnt to a crisp on the outside and when you stuck your fork into it, raw batter oozed everywhere. Not wanting to starve, I hustled over to the Captain's camp and found him sitting in one of his handmade chairs, cooking over the fire, skillfully making little pancake animals.

Often when I recall the things I did that were "memory builders," they include either one or both of my brothers. It is at those moments that I become incredibly thankful to be one of the Moser boys.

CHAPTER 16.

HAPPY TRAILS

Roy Rogers and Dale Evans would close their show each week singing, "Happy trails to you, until we meet again." Those words come to my young mind as the Moser Gang rides into the sunset. The imaginations of these five boys that you have been reading about are what I have done my best to bring back to life. That span in the timeline of our lives is so precious. There is an innocence and purity that can only be captured in the hearts and lives of those who are not afraid to dream.

In conclusion, there is the honest question: What happened to those boys after they grew

CHAPTER SIXTEEN

up? There are more stories. They got older, of course, and that next stage of life began to happen. Oh, the deer hunting stories (those are the ones my own son loves to hear about over and over), the high school years of hot cars, four-wheel drives, motorcycles, guns, and guitars. But that's for another time, another set of adventures put to pen and paper.

So, where are we today? One of the members sadly has passed away, taking with him his version of each chapter you have read. A couple of the boys, obviously much older now, are still working, and a couple of us have retired from the daily routine of work but are still living out our older dreams and imaginations.

Captain, my older brother who brought back to life the old truck, went on to become one of the best mechanics in the valley. I know this to be true because he just came out to revive my dying tractor. Red Boots, my younger brother, still gets referred to with that nickname and it still holds all the respect and honor that it deserves.

THE MOSER GANG

As for me, the Christian ministry called me out in my early twenties, and I still serve in that capacity today. I call on my memories of the Moser Gang often as I share and teach about those days of adventure and exploits that being a member of the gang brings back to light. As shared early on, the imaginations and dreams of young children are essential to the saying of Jesus when he stated, "Except you be like children, you cannot see the Kingdom of God."

It is our ability to use our imaginations that we learned as children, along with the holy spirit within us, that reveals the unseen realm of the Kingdom of God. The "happy trails" I now walk are in anticipation of meeting my Lord Jesus when he returns to gather his saints together to spend the rest of eternity with him. Until then, the building that is now taking place is the building of the family of God… the most exciting project of all!

"If there is one thing that children are known for, it is love for adventure. And maturity, for us, is to be childlike. All of this speaks of the whole realm of adventure and creativity that is to be associated with following Christ."[1]

---

[1] Bill Johnson, *Open Heavens*, p. 249.

ABOUT THE AUTHOR

Bob Moser grew up working in the sawmill where he played as a boy. During his childhood and early adulthood, he lived and worked on the very land that was settled by his ancestors who came west on the Oregon Trail. Those early years laid the foundation for his life as an imaginer, a dreamer, a builder, and a visionary.

In 1975 he began a journey that put him on a pathway of Christian service that he is still pursuing to this very day. Bob and his first wife, Cindee, served God across the United States from Maine to California and then returned to Oregon to raise a family of four wonderful children.

Bob remarried after the passing of his first wife, and now he and Trish live on the Good

Seed Ranch in the foothills of the Coast Range Mountains in Oregon. As ordained Christian ministers, they travel and teach as well as host local gatherings. Their home is a place of inspiration, rest and refreshing, laughter and joy for family and friends. Their land also serves as a refuge for a variety of wildlife, including deer and herds of elk passing through.

Bob and Trish delight in spending time with their blended family of children: Hannah and Clinton, Rachel, Sayde and Bill, Andrew and Kristen, Rebekah, and all the wonderful grandchildren: Sam, Elly, Lucy, Grace, Gus, Ruby, Gideon, and Jeremiah.

The Good Seed Ranch Home

MOSER GANG GALLERY

The hollow tree.

Okay boys... Here is the plan.

Younger brother with the four-footed leader of the Moser Gang.

I tell you little brother, this dog knows stuff.

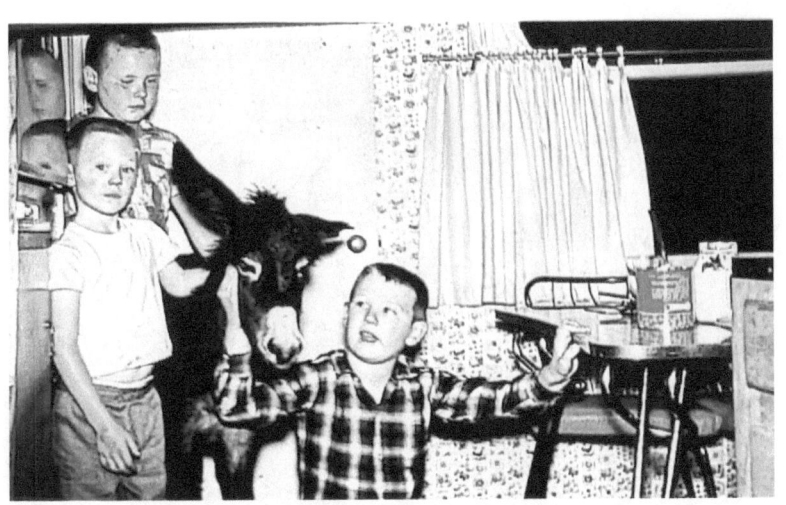

Mom, can our new friend come over for dinner?

Covered a lot of sheep trail miles on that bike.

Brothers and bikes pedaling into adventure.

Summer is over. Time to grab our lunch boxes and get an education.

Band of brothers.

Original sawmill in Hoskins.

Wigwam burner... End of a sawmill era.

Mill pond my dad and I took a dip into.

Hoskins Lumber Company on a winter's day.

Papa getting ready for a threshing bee.

Three generations of Moser Gang DNA.

Papa had a giant heart, giant hands and a giant shadow.

Mom and Dad.

www.ingramcontent.com/pod-product-compliance
Lightning Source LLC
Chambersburg PA
CBHW020654060526
44119CB00069B/31